DELAYED

NOT DENIED, NOR DERAILED

CHOSEN TO RELEASE KEYS FOR VICTORY

ANGELA IVORY

DELAYED

NOT DENIED, NOR DERAILED

CHOSEN TO RELEASE KEYS FOR VICTORY

ANGELA IVORY

Delayed not Denied, nor Derailed – Chosen to Release Keys of Victory

Published by Never A-Mis Enterprises, LLC
P.O. Box 2298
Byron, GA 31008-2298
www.neveramisenterprises.com

ISBN: 9798990833708

Repentance Revival Prayer – From Prayer Mountain in Australia – Prayer Downloads - Pastor Robert Clancy

FOREWORD

Some are called to genuinely make a difference. Angela Ivory is one of those who, through her writing conveys this truth. John writes, "He is the Lord of lords and the King of kings: and they that are with him are called, and chosen, and faithful (Revelations 17:14 KJV)." Join Angela as she takes you on her journey of being chosen by God to release keys for victory.

While the enemy tried to delay her purpose – she shows that being delayed does not mean you are denied. God chooses us in the "furnace of affliction (Isaiah 48:10 KJV)" to refine us for service. The Psalmist said that Joseph's feet were hurt with fetters, and he was laid in iron, "until the time that his word came: the Word of the Lord tried him (Psalms 105:19 KJV)."

As she gives you keys for victory – The idea is that you must first be healed from issues and hurt from the past. Healing and deliverance are necessary if we are going to move on. As you read this book, pray that you hear the Holy Spirit (the heart of what she is saying) and sidestep all derailment attempts by the adversary.

Pastor Melvin Womack

THE INTRODUCTION

When the Lord made me, He made me with a purpose. He made me a wife, a friend, a daughter and more. He made me a warrior with purpose and assignments. God formed me in my mother's womb; and He had a conversation with me.

The enemy's strategy has always been to position himself so he could challenge the truth (God's Word) God spoke to us His children. He wants to derail us as we pursue the fulfillment of the Word in our lives. He did it in The Garden of Eden with Adam & Eve. He even tempted Jesus while He was in the wilderness; rest assured he will try the same strategy against you.

The enemy tried to delay, derail, and detour me from my purpose incredibly early in my life when I was a little girl, and has persistently continued. I remember waking up in the middle of the night, and when I looked out my window, and I saw a figure standing there. Little did I know then that it was a monitoring spirit. I would cry, my mother would come in and console me every time. I would ask, "Mom, don't you see the man at the window?" Later in my life, my mother received a prophecy about me. Now that she has transitioned, I now know she understood what the Woman of God told her. She said, "Keep her in white." It is very befitting that I am in white on the cover of this book. Even as I am writing, Holy Spirit reminded me that I was in white on the cover of my first book.

I received a similar prophecy about three years ago from; at the time, my Pastor/Prophet that released, "I see you on a cover of a book dressed in white with a red background." You are seeing the manifestation of that prophecy RIGHT NOW! Also, within the last year of drafting this book, I am now under an Apostolic leadership that has confirmed along with the prophet that there is another book to be written soon. In total, I have been working on this book over ten years. When I say working on it, I mean I have taken my experiences from the time I knew God called me to ministry, until this very day.

I have been chosen by God to release keys for victory. The adversary thought he could delay or derail my purpose knowing there was no way he could deny it! It wasn't until I truly understood that the enemy could not deny my purpose, there was a definitive shift and turnaround in my life. Throughout this book, I am going to share my journey; from the beginning when I understood the Lord called me to ministry, and where I am currently in my assignment. I am purposefully being transparent, so can I encourage and inspire those of you who have experienced some of the same trials, setbacks, and disappointments I have experienced; and how to deal with the pain.

You may have also been delayed, but certainly not denied. I am here to let you know the derailment can be destroyed. I pray you are set free, delivered and healed.

During the process of the Lord restoring you, I pray you will give our Lord - Jesus Christ ALL the Glory, Honor, and Praise due to His Holy name.

Delay - make (someone or something) Late or slow; a period by which something is late or postponed.

Denied - state that one refuses to admit the truth or existence of; refuse to give or grant (something requested or desired) to (someone).
Restoration - the action of returning something to a former owner, place, or condition; the return of a hereditary monarch to a throne; a head of state to government, or a regime of power.

Recompense – make amends to (someone) for loss or harm suffered; compensate; compensation or reward given for loss or harm suffered or effort made.

Recompense (King James Dictionary) - to repay; reward; restore. "The Lord rewarded me according to my righteousness; according to the cleanliness of my hands hath He RECOMPENSED me. For I have kept the ways of the Lord and have not wickedly left from my God."

"Instead of your shame you will receive a double portion, and instead of disgrace you will rejoice in your inheritance. And so you will inherit a double portion in your land, and everlasting joy will be yours (Isaiah

61:7 ***NIV).*** *"* The enemy tried to delay; and most certainly could not deny me. I am believing God for restoration, recompense, and receiving my double portion. I believe God will even restore everything the enemy ***THOUGHT*** he stole. On this journey you will read how I learned how to break the cycles & stop going in circles.

TABLE OF CONTENTS

TABLE OF CONTENTS

Chapter One

THE CALL.

Let me walk you through my journey... I was not aware I was called by God until after my husband and I remarried; after being divorced a year; and being married nineteen years! Once we were reunited in marriage, I learned he needed a kidney transplant.

In the latter part of 2012, headed into 2013, I was afforded the opportunity to travel to Memphis, TN for a business trip. While there I was able to connect with a few ladies I met on social media a few months prior. A certain lady I was connected to in business introduced me to a group of ladies who were fasting online. I joined them with their fast called "Diva Fast for Finances." Even though I do not associate or consider myself a diva, I know and am assured that I am a Woman of God! The same business trip I was invited to attend was the hometown of the other three ladies I met months earlier in the fast. It gets better ... later I found Nicole was the founder of the fast. She had other ladies providing support with encouragement to the ladies during the fast. There were more ladies supporting the participants of the fast from all over the globe with encouragement. However, the

Lord DIVINELY CONNECTED me to Nicole, Jessica and Roshunda.

Once the fast was completed, around three the next morning I was awakened by the Holy Spirit, and I went into the bathroom, which was my prayer closet at that time. As I inquired of the Holy Spirit, He instructed me to sow into the founder of the fast. In my mind I am like, “I don’t know who the founder is.” The Holy Spirit led me to encourage the other ladies to consider sowing if they received anything that transformed their lives during the fast. Long story short, that caught the attention of one of the supporting ladies named Roshunda. She then contacted Nicole, to let her know someone was looking for her. Roshunda connected me to Nicole, who was the founder. I was able to talk the person whom I was led to sow into. I asked, and as led by the Holy Spirit, I sent the amount I was instructed to send. I found out later that the seed I sowed was exactly what she needed; plus, she would be the one to reveal to me I was called by God to "feed His sheep".

Pay close attention ... I was invited to a business meeting by the leading couple in the organization I was a part of ... I then reach out to Nicole, who then in turn reached out to Jessica and Roshunda to see if we could all meet for dinner. God has a way of getting you where you need to be when you need to be there!!!! As soon as I sat down at the table, Jessica at once began to prophesy ... She told me about my father and how I would lead him to Christ (there is more to that story I will share later). Jessica was on point with the prophesy, even as to what is currently going on in my life right now.

KEY **-** Sometimes God will use His vessels to release a "Word". It may not happen right away, just hold on until manifestation comes. The prophecy about my father happened several months later after talking to the women of God from Memphis.

After dinner, Nicole and I went back to the hotel and sat down in the lobby to talk. We began to discuss the business I was a part of. She began to release a Word of Knowledge concerning the company I was connected to, which really got my attention. She went on to say, "But God says to "feed His sheep." Its 3am again, having this discussion. I knew enough about the Word to know exactly what that meant.

A little later when I went up to the room, I asked God to confirm what was said. I went to sleep for a few hours and as I was beginning to prepare for the day, while I was in worship, the Lord showed me an open vision of myself standing on a platform preaching. I could hear myself saying, "It's time for us to stop playing church." The Lord confirmed what the young lady spoke to me. I have heard most run from their calling. I was not going to run. I did not understand how this was going to come about, but I had enough trust and faith in

God that He would lead and direct me. I noticed the Lord began to place me around prophetic people and placing prophetic people around me. I never chased after a prophetic word or go looking for one. I penned this book in 2023, but I can remember many occurrences that have happened years before because of the way the Lord orchestrated these divine moments. It still amazes me how the Lord had to take me to an entirely different state to give me a message.

The prophecy about my father ... Prior to going to see my father, the Holy Spirit let me know he would pass away; I just did not know the exact time. The Holy Spirit allowed me the opportunity to share Christ with my father in an unconventional way when I went to see him. Again ... God has a way of getting you where you need to be when you need to be there!

When I first heard the news of my father's passing, I was distraught because I thought I did not do what the Lord asked me to do. The Holy Spirit reminded me after I shared with my father about Mark needing a kidney transplant, and that by faith I believed he would get it. Even though our conversation was unconventional, it was exactly what my father needed to hear because of what he has always seen happen with people who need kidney transplants. OHHH but I believed God!! My faith led me to let my father know that Mark would receive what he needed, AND he would live. I PRAISE GOD with this testimony BECAUSE WITHIN ONE YEAR OF THE DIAGNOSIS, AT THE END OF THAT YEAR WHEN HE REACHED THE POINT OF HAVING TO BE PLACED ON DIALYSIS. HE RECEIVED A PERFECT MATCH AND NEVER HE NEVER

STARTED DIALYSIS. However, my father died three months prior to Mark receiving his new kidney.

Mark's mom was diagnosed with kidney disease, even though she did not pass away from it, Mark inherited the disease. Later I will talk about sickness & disease that need to be broken in our family's bloodline.

Chapter Two

Be led by the Spirit.

When I returned to Georgia after being gone for seven days, my corporate worship experience was quite different. This was the first time I had ever experienced this type of Holy Ghost encounter. While in worship, at the church I was attending at that time, I began to speak in tongues. The church I worshiped at consisted of guitars, keyboards, and all kinds of instruments; and was very loud. As I began to speak in tongues, my tongues shut down the music that was being played during worship. Because of the interruption, one of the ushers came over to try and settle me down.

When the usher came and she touched me, the Holy Spirit touched her, and she began to speak in tongues. My tongues needed interpretation. Order in the house of God would be that an interpretation would follow so there was not any confusion ... The leader moves forward, mounted the platform, and began to talk about healing. Right before the Man of God stood up, the Holy Spirt said, "Walk to the front of the church and sit on the front row." I heard what the Holy Spirt said to me, but the weight of His Glory was resting on me so heavily so that I could not move. In my head I was conversating with the Holy Spirit. I said, "I cannot move, You are too heavy on me. Can You let up a little and I can go, as I laughed to myself!" As I am simultaneously having a conversation with the Holy Spirit and preparing to move like instructed, the leader began to go over some of the same scriptures the Lord gave me to read about healing. Now, keep in mind, Mark needed a kidney transplant, so I was praying the same healing scriptures.

After I positioned myself on the front row, there were a few people that tried to move me. I refused to be moved. I continued to tell them, "I am not doing this own my own. This is God and I refuse to move." Even with all the movement of the people trying to move me off the front row, it never became a distraction. As I listened to the Leader, it was as if God gave him a download of what I had been praying. There is no way to make this stuff up! Unfortunately, because I did not fully understand the anointing that was on my life others could see; I did not have it all figured out, so it allowed for a door to be opened for the enemy. My ignorance was the open door. The Bible says, "My people are destroyed from lack of knowledge ... (Hosea 4:6a *NIV)*."

KEY – When you do not know who you are or what your identity is in Jesus Christ, it can open the door for you to be led in the wrong direction. Even though it may not be intentional to give you inaccurate information, sometimes people will be used to withhold information. If they are not led by the Spirit of God, they are being led by their flesh they can mislead you and you will become stagnant. To be stagnant as defined earlier, is not to move, not to grow, not to flourish or flow. It is just like someone giving you a prophetic word and it is from a familiar spirit; their flesh. Because the prophecy came from their flesh, it leads us down the wrong road for a lengthy period until someone comes to break you out of a trance.

Soon after that Holy Ghost experience I had during the worship service; the Holy Spirit led me to speak to the Man of God; the bishop. I started out by sharing with him what I experienced in Memphis with the three young ladies. The wisdom Bishop shared with me was encouraging. He told me to continue to obey the leading of the Holy Spirit. I did not share the information about the open vision early morning while in Memphis. Before I went to meet with Bishop, a wise woman of God said to me, "Your shepherd will know. You will not have to explain everything that has happened." I received the wisdom Bishop shared with me in that meeting. By the time I reached the parking lot after our meeting, the Holy Spirit whispered, "Your season is over here."

This was the second time the Holy Spirit told me it was time to leave a particular ministry, the first time I was attending a Baptist church. When I left the Baptist church, it was a process of instructions I obeyed. First, He led me to step away from the choir and praise team ... I thought I was just taking a break. A week later after attending service, I started to question why I was even there. One of the older saints walked up to me – she saw a perplexed look on my face and said, "Just do what the Holy Spirit is leading you to do." When I moved to Georgia from Louisiana, I already experienced a church that believed in the five-fold; Apostles, Prophets, Evangelists, Pastors, and Teachers were in operation. Being at the Baptist church was a like taking a step backwards. I am not criticizing the Baptist church because I received my foundation, but there is a big difference. When you know God is leading you, you cannot worry about others are going to think or say. You have to let God be God and know He will be your Vindicator. After all, no matter where you are located, we are the Body of Christ in the Kingdom of God.

KEY – When you are led by the Spirit to leave a ministry, there will be fiery darts and false accusations thrown at you.

"*The LORD is for me, so I will have no fear. What can mere people do to me?* [7] *Yes, the LORD is for me; he will help me. I will look in triumph at those who hate me.* [8] *It is better to take refuge in the LORD than to trust in people (Psalms 118:6 – 8* ***NLT)****.*"

28 "Don't be afraid of those who want to kill your body; they cannot touch your soul. Fear only God, who can destroy both soul and body in hell (Matthew 10:28 ***NLT)****."*

Chapter Three

The next assignment.

My training took place in different ministries. It was just like I was attending school, and I learned a lot in each place. Throughout my journey, when individuals leave, leaders may not view it as the person was in "training" there, and it is time for them to move on. Now mind you, I have seen plenty of people come and go, yet some people you did not hear anything about when they left the ministry. In my case, there were a lot of side-eyes and whispering from the Body of Believers. Not at this particular church, but one I will share another experience about. I also experienced word curses being spoken to me that I had to quickly renounce. Unfortunately, at this particular church I saw a lot of things behind the scenes. I was taught a lot of what to do, what not to do, and how to treat people. Again, this was the method of schooling God had for me. In the first book I co-authored, I mentioned there was not a cookie cutter way for God to shift you in life. My process may not be like yours, but if you find or have found yourself in this situation let me encourage you to move when God says to move. Be obedient to God. Because of the Apostolic anointing I now understand that rests upon my life, it makes sense why I would want to put things in order behind the scenes.

While in "training" I did not know who I was by titles, other than minister. Neither was I recognized in the other ministries I attended. I learned how to recognize who I was without the leadership of the ministries acknowledging it. When it was time for me to leave this ministry, I was asked, "Did anyone ever tell you that you were a prophet?" No one other than the ministry I am currently attending now has ever spoke about an Apostolic prophetic anointing on my life.

I found out about the apostolic anointing by spending time alone with my Lord and Savior during my wilderness experience. Later, God used other men and women of God outside of the middle Georgia to confirm what He showed me to help me on this journey. Please understand it has nothing to do with stroking another's ego, but it is about building people. Please understand there is a big difference of you being called a minster to preach the Word of God and being a prophet. I will not even being to touch on the Apostolic calling. It makes perfect sense for leadership to be able to recognize the leadership in others. I learned people cannot teach you what is beyond them or there are spiritual reasons as to why they were not able to recognize the gifting. There were a few other leaders who were local (none of which were my coverings) that recognized the anointing on my life.

The ignorance I had in the beginning of learning who I was did open doors. One of the biggest lessons I learned in this ministry is about the spirits of offense, jealousy, competition, and pride.

KEY – Seek the Lord and ask Him to show you who you are in the Spirit, and then you will understand and know what type of ministry you need to sit under; even if it is for a short period of time. It is important to know who you are submitted to and who they are submitted to. I was able to recognize a shift in the ministry when the ministry's covering changed. It became more about business, than it was about souls. If people are telling you must stay connected to a church because you need a covering, hear this ... Our Father made sure we were triple covered. First, we are covered by God; then our natural father, or our husbands (if you are married); and lastly a spiritual covering. If the latter two are not in position, do not worry, God always covers you. By no means am I saying you do not need accountability or spiritual guidance, it is needed.

DOUBLE KEY – AGAIN **...** It is particularly important to be led by the Spirit where you fellowship and making sure you are under the correct covering. You should be in a place where you receive correction and encouragement. We do not know everything, so we should remain teachable. If you find yourself at a place and no one is correcting you; shedding light on sin with and love, that is a red flag. Most people in leadership are not always liked, and it comes with the territory. Those in leadership correct, rebuke, and encourage. Correction is necessary for growth without an attitude. *"I solemnly urge you in the presence of God and Jesus Christ, who will someday judge the living and the dead when He returns to set up His Kingdom: Preach the Word of God. Be prepared, whether it is favorable or* *not. Patiently correct, rebuke, and encourage your people with good teaching (2 Timothy 4:1-2* ***NLT****).*"

Chapter Four

More lessons learned.

(How I identify different spirits in operation.)

I digress back to the lessons about the different spirits I encountered and what I learned. As I am being transparent, I was naive and I did not expect to learn the lessons l learned within the body of believers, let alone from leaders. I expected a higher standard of living as the Word commands. "*So, you must live as God's obedient children. Do not slip back into your old ways of living to satisfy your own desires. You did not know any better then. But now you must be holy in everything you do, just as God who chose you is holy. For the Scriptures say, "You must be holy because I am Holy." And remember that the heavenly Father to whom you pray has no favorites. He will judge or reward you according to what you do. So, you must live in reverent fear of him during your time here as "temporary residents." For you know that God paid a ransom to save you from the empty life you inherited from you ancestors. And it was not paid with mere gold or silver, which lose their value. It was the precious blood of Christ, the sinless, spotless Lamb of God (1 Peter 1:14 – 19* ***NLT****)."*

When I refer to leaders, it is not just the pastor of the church, it is also anyone that has been appointed a leader within church. If you are like me, I questioned if they were so close knitted within leadership that the Pastors did not recognize their behavior? If you spend time with people, you will notice different things about them, good or bad. Just because you pastor a church or have a title, it does not exclude you from having strongholds and needing deliverance. Every time I went on another assignment, I began to see the same spirit (behavior) working in different people. Continuing to see the same spirit allowed me to identify them and how to pray targeted prayers of intercession as led by the Lord.

I want to make it perfectly clear that as I am sharing my life and how I got to where I am today, I am NOT holding any grudges; I am NOT walking in unforgiveness; and I am NOT holding any bitterness towards those who allowed the enemy to use them. My honest prayer for all that are in authority would live tranquil, undisturbed lives, as we worship God with godliness and pure hearts. Many do not understand the persecution I have endured when I said, "Yes!" The enemy thought if he could sabotage my life,

I would not fulfill my purpose to cause damage to the kingdom of darkness. One of the biggest lessons I learned was not to allow the spirit of offense to overtake me, and to forgive people. My heart had to be completely clear BEFORE releasing this book.

As I look back over my journey, my life reminds me of a couple of people in the Bible: Jeremiah, Joseph, and David ... Jeremiah was called to lead a stubborn people, so his work was to pluck up, tear down, and build again. His message was to repent and return to God, or they would be punished. He suffered opposition; slander; he was mocked; rejected by friends and family, false prophets, and priests. He received threats; they tried to muzzle his mouth; he was watched by people waiting to see him fall. But God ... "*But the Lord stands beside me like a great warrior. Before him my persecutors will stumble. They cannot defeat me. They will fail and be thoroughly humiliated. Their dishonor will never be forgotten (Jeremiah 20:11* ***NLT****).*"

On to Joseph ... Jacob's most beloved son was Joseph. Since he was the favorite, he was hated by his envious brother's. The hatred and jealousy of Joseph's brother became more obvious when Jacob gifted him a "coat of many colors." They began to plot to kill him and threw him into cistern to die. Death was not Joseph's portion, so they sold him to a party of Ishmaelites or Midianites, who took him to Egypt.

I have three natural brothers. Two of my brothers are my stepbrothers because we do not have the same father; and my other brother and I have both same mother and father. I never thought my brothers would have a reason to be envious or jealous of me. I found out, after talking to my oldest brother, he was upset when my mom had me; not to do me harm, but it did display a spirit of jealousy. Maybe he thought because I was the only girl, I would get more attention. He never mentioned feeling the same way when my brother who was born five years before me. My mother miscarried a baby girl before I was born. Me and my oldest brother have a beautiful loving relationship. He is constantly reminding me that he is the oldest. I remind him that the Word of God says last shall be first! We often joke around with each other; but I do not have an interest in his birthright.

I do not want to walk in his shoes as being the first born, and he cannot walk in my shoes as being the last.

On my journey as being called to ministry, I later realized I had sisters and brothers in Christ that allowed the spirit of jealousy and envy they carried, use them. I did not share my dreams like Joseph did. Even though I did not share my dreams, they could see where God was taking me, or the gifts within me before I really knew myself. If there was a seed of envy or jealousy within them, it became a part of the devil's plot. The spirit of jealousy, envy, strife, and competition does not care who it uses, and it will use a willing vessel that has seeds planted in them which came from past trauma, generational curses, and need deliverance. It took me a while to wrap my head around the fact that the very same people that were in place to push or lead me into my destiny, were the very same people that were in place to derail, hinder or try to kill what God purposed for me.

KEY – The Holy Spirit knows how to teach you what you need to know. A year after I was instructed to leave a particular ministry, I had a dream that helped me identify the spirit of envy and jealousy ...

Once I learned the tactics and schemes of the enemy ... it was on! I learned how to forgive those who mistreated me and mishandled me. I had several opportunities to get it right. The saddest realization of this lesson was that this behavior came from several leaders, and people with influence. I wrestled with learning how to truly forgive those individuals. I say wrestle because of one incident the person went out of their way to hurt me. They apologized, however even after they apologized, other things happened because of their actions to provoke me. I had to apologize for my actions. Even after they apologized, I still wrestled with what they did. It was hard to get over even though I knew the words that came out of my mouth, there was still something in my heart. I had a dream concerning a particular minister, and in the dream, they were trying to force me to apologize even though they were the one that did awful things to me and came after me.

I realized there still was unforgiveness in my heart after I had the dream a year after everything happened. I had to go back and consult the Lord about the residue that was still in my heart. When I asked the Lord why I was having the dream. He gave me *"Matthew 6:14 – 15* ***NIV*** **...** *For if you forgive other people when they sin (trespass) against you, your heavenly Father will also forgive you. So, in other words if you do not forgive others of their sins, your Father will not forgive your sins."*

I need forgiveness from the Lord! Once I read the Scripture, it was so impactful that it broke the power of offense, and I was able to forgive them. Even though Holy Spirit gave me the Scripture years ago,

I needed to revisit it because the Lord took me a step further. He explained to me where the behavior from the other person came from. He gave me, *"For where there is jealousy and envy there's all manners of evil."* The Lord let me know there was a seed already inside of this person. They were carrying around jealousy, but they wanted to seem as if they were wise. *"Do you want to be counted wise, to build a reputation for wisdom? Here is what you do: Live well, live wisely, live humbly. It is the way you live, not the way you talk, that counts. Mean-spirited ambition is not wisdom. Boasting that you are wise is not wisdom. Twisting the truth to make yourselves sound wise is not wisdom. It is the furthest thing from wisdom—it is animal cunning, devilish plotting. Whenever you are trying to look better than others or get the better of others, things fall apart, and everyone ends up at the others' throats. Real wisdom, God's wisdom, begins with a holy life and is characterized by having a good relationship with others. It is gentle and reasonable, overflowing with mercy and blessings, not hot one day and cold the next, not two-faced. You can develop a healthy, robust community that lives right with God and enjoy its results only if you do the demanding work of having a good relationship with each other, Treating each other with dignity and honor (James 3:13 – 18* ***MSG****).”*

As much as I tried to see the good in people, I learned they may be in a place of leadership, family, or considered a friend, the enemy is always trying to destroy and hinder us from completing our assignments.

KEY – These are agents, but we cannot allow the spirit of offense stop us. It will eventually turn into bitterness, and you will start acting just like them because of needing deliverance. When I understood this, it was easy for me to pray for them, and that they would get healing and deliverance from whatever stronghold has them bound; in their lives, or in their bloodline. Satan and his cohort's job is not only to keep you off track from the original instruction from the Lord. Their job is also to keep confusion between our brothers and sisters in Christ.

Let us talk about David ... David respected King Saul, but he would flee from his grips. David had several opportunities to kill King Saul, but he would not do it. King Saul was so envious and jealous of David.

Remember, *"For we wrestle not against flesh and blood, but against principalities, against powers, against the rulers of the darkness of this world, against spiritual wickedness in high places (Eph 6:12***KJV**)." God revealed the spirit of jealousy and pride within King Saul. The Word says, "*When the men were returning home after David had killed the Philistine, the women came out from all the towns of Israel to meet King Saul with singing and dancing, with joyful songs and with timbrels and lyres.* [7] *As they danced, they sang: "Saul has slain his thousands, and David his tens of* *thousands." [8] Saul was incredibly angry; this refrain displeased him. "They have credited David with tens of thousands," he thought, "but me with only thousands. What more can he get but the kingdom?" [9] And from that time on Saul kept a close eye on David (1 Samuel 18:6 – 9* ***NIV****)."* This story was an example of offense or being offended. The spirit of offense is the bait of satan. He wants you to be offended by people.

KEY – When you hold offence it blocks your blessings and opens a door for a spirit of infirmities (sickness), rejection, and depression. Before long, you are caught in a cycle. The enemy also comes to wear out the Saints so he can easily defeat you. He wants us to give up and quit. If you quit, you will not complete your assignment. David could have become bitter and offended because of Saul's actions. I did not forget what happened, I just did not allow my spirit to be contaminated. I understood this was happening as part of my process to recognized different spirits. I gleamed from my past experiences. Receiving revelation helped increase the spirit of discernment.

Chapter Five

The wilderness.

I was led to disconnect from the local body and stay home two separate times. The Holy Spirit led me to five different ministries. Eventually the Lord connected me with other women of God that was on a similar path. We learned from one another. Even though we were not on the same level, we had each other's back; we covered each other in prayer and shared our walk with each other – the good the bad and the ugly. When one of us could not hear God clearly, He used each one of as a mouthpiece for one another. This was a glimpse of what the Body of the Christ should look like if we supported one another and build each other instead of tearing each other down or competing. We were not on the same level, as I mentioned before, but we had the same goal in mind, and that was to please our Father. It was a time to study to show myself approved; to develop a stronger relationship with the Lord. It was time to live my life in strict obedience to God. It was not the time for me to worry about following someone else's curriculum or expectations of what they thought I was supposed to be within the four walls of the church. It was time for me to really know who God was to me and to know His heart ... it was time to completely die to self. It was in the wilderness where King David trained. My wilderness continued to be my training ground.

Chapter Six

Betrayal; Forgiveness; Freedom & Blessings.

During this period of my journey, I had the opportunity to get to know God even the more, while at the same time learning lessons of how the enemy used people; even my sisters and brothers in Christ. When the enemy has a plan to keep you from your purpose, he does not care who he uses. He will use any individual to distract you if they have an accessible open door. I found myself praying more for the people I knew were sent by God, but the deception from the enemy caused them to disconnect. I knew they were purposely in my life for more than a season.

My prayer life increased more, which gave me more insight into how to intercede for my sisters for forgiveness and grace to be extended to them. No one is exempt from needing deliverance. I also understood the enemy was trying to entangle me once again with a spirit of rejection. I am thankful I was able to recognize the enemy's tactic, and that I was truly delivered from that spirit. The adversary would have wanted nothing more than for me to throw away, give up, or turn my back on them. I was hurt by their behavior, and I missed the closeness of my sisters, but I understood the cause of the separation. Remember, *"Your hand-to-hand combat is not with human beings, but with the highest principalities and authorities working in rebellion under the heavenly realms. For they are a powerful class of demon-gods and evil spirits that hold this mysterious world in bondage.* [13]*Because of this, you must wear all the armor that God provides so you're protected as you confront the slanderer, for you are destined for all things and will rise victorious (Eph. 6:12-13* ***TPT****)."*

Because I was able to recognize what the enemy was trying to do, I was determined not to leave any soldier behind. I continued to pray as led by the Lord. Fortunately, after a few years, the Lord restored our relationships. During my intercession and prayers for others, the Lord blessed my family. He did wonderful things, which increased my faith even more. I so enjoyed the freedom of worshipping the Lord without having to be on a schedule; not having to be at a certain place at a certain time, and not a specific day of the week. The Lord had given me instructions a couple of years back to walk away from a fourteen-year career in the medical field and led me back to culinary arts. By this time, on my journey I understood I was called to several mountains of influence: one was in ministry AIM (Angela Ivory Ministries was birthed); the second was in the marketplace. The Lord afforded me many opportunities to minister to people outside of the four walls of the church in the marketplace as an entrepreneur. I understand it is having an Apostolic anointing in the marketplace.

After my three-year journey, the Lord led me back to another ministry, where I was able to put into action the things I learned in the last three years. Even though my discernment had increased, I still needed assistance after being in place a year at this ministry. The Lord sent a woman of God to bring to my attention that I still needed to dive deeper into prayer. The question in my mind was, "If I am sitting under leadership, why wasn't this addressed or brought to my attention? Why wasn't I corrected by leadership, or encouraged to stir up my prayer life?" This brings me back to what I shared earlier about red flags and correction causes growth. The Word says the Lord will give us shepherds after His own heart. I quickly realized that unfortunately, just like the case with my sisters, the Lord was opening my eyes to see there is a need for ALL to be delivered; even leadership. I also realized that people have placed some leaders on a pedestal that they should not be on. And some leaders have allowed themselves to be placed on pedestals. Love for people can have you blinded, and you cannot see the spirits that are working behind the face or title. I found myself seeing different spirits working in people that could 'pray the house down' or preach a great or motivational message. I also found myself saying when I recognize certain things, this person or that person needs to be delivered ... I still had no full idea what I was saying!

By this time on my journey, I was now a published author; I had an interview on a TV show in Atlanta. Shortly after, I was the host on my own talk show – Destiny Helpers, which allowed me to gain experience of being on the radio and tv. The third mountain of influence for me is media. Those experiences were the beginning of being in the media ... the rest has yet to be told.

My obedience to the Lord was far more important than anything or anyone. If the Lord sent me to deliver a 'Word' to a leader, then I said whatever the Lord led me to say. I could not worry how they felt about it, I had to release it. I have two names; Samuel and Eli. They are examples in the Bible of Samuel being younger than Eli but having to give a hard 'Word' to Eli. I did not have to give a leader a 'Word' about their seed doing or saying anything against God, and them not controlling the seed. However, it was a hard "Word "about a different situation.

Another opportunity came of me being led by the Holy Spirit to bring a situation to another leader's attention. Yet again, the correction was rejected, and I was labeled as being rebellious. I was not only tested in ministry, but I was also tested in the marketplace. God placed me in the mountain of influence. He would show me how things needed correction. I also was put in similar situations in various places, and they were not popular in the least. I simply wanted to live a life consecrated to Him. He was showing me that everybody was not there in their walk with Him. He also showed me that Leviathan, the king of pride was working in a lot of people. Although I respected the leader, and I really thought this time I had a place I could settle in ... The Lord was showing me differently; it was another place of training to sharpen my discernment. I had to obey God. The Lord in His infinite wisdom shifted me again. I did not move until He told me to do so. I left with the Lord's orders, and knowing I was being obedient to God.

KEY – The Lord will not allow you to stay in a place where your gift is not received. God has a way of separating you from people, but you must be willing to be open to hear, pray and move when the Lord tells you to go.

When led by the Holy Spirit, I disconnected from the fourth ministry, and I found myself just wanting to be somewhere I could be received and loved without any hidden agendas. At this particular ministry love was there, the Word was there, the Holy Spirit was there, it just was not the Apostolic covering I needed. When the pandemic happened in 2020, I had no problem being at home because I was already worshipping on my own and hiding the Word in my heart.

As I stated previously, people need deliverance, and I did not know how it was going to come. I was referred to a deliverance ministry in Louisiana, by one of my cousins. Even though it was so far away, when you are wholeheartedly pursuing God and desire to be obedient to where He is leading you to connect, you just obey and trust Him. God knows exactly what we need and when we need it. I was only there for a brief period, but I found a different atmosphere of worship and went through deliverance myself! PRAISE THE LORD!!! While I was there, I received a lot of answers to the questions as to why I kept making statements about people needing deliverance. Louisiana, as well as other states that have hurricanes, but this ministry was shifted to a different location, but not before I got what I needed. God shifted me and gave them new instructions. God gave the leaders instructions to pray for those who were connected to the ministry. One of the prophet/pastors prayed with each one that desired prayer. The leader released, "There is a ministry in my area for me to connect to. She instructed me not to move until I was certain it was the right connection."

KEY – Let us be clear ... Absolutely no one or ministry is perfect. You need to be connected under the right leadership. For instance, if you need an apostolic way of teaching, you need to sit under an apostle versus a pastor. The pastor is submitted under the apostle, but you may need to in closer proximity of the Apostolic leader. You cannot expect to be taught something from someone who does not have the anointing to lead you.

I worshipped, prayed, and waited six months before the Lord sent a man of God to release a 'Word' to me. It took another three months before I was led by the Holy

Spirit to find out what ministry in Georgia the man of God worshipped at, the Lord used to give me a Word. It took a total of nine months for the Lord to answer my question about where the ministry I was to connect to located in Georgia. By then, I was already learning more about deliverance. Once I connected to the ministry, it was like a breath of fresh air. I say that because there was not any 'sugar coating' of the Word, and I loved it! Sin was called sin, and there is no way around it. The wages of sin is death.

KEY – Correction should be found along with love at churches. The Holy Spirit must be in control. You should be able to follow the leader, as he/she follows Christ. If you see something that is not right, pray and cover them (you will see a change if they are led by the Spirit of God). Being connected to this ministry has helped me re-align myself and confirmed my identity in Christ. I also recognized this too was an assignment. Being connected to the other ministries and understanding more of the call on my life taught me that if the Lord gave me instructions to move, or it was time to be released, I would have to go. As of right now, I still planted in the same ministry.

After a time of fellowship and worshipping; following His instructions; and taking delight in Lord led me to more breakthroughs in my life. He gave me some of the desires of my heart; but there was still work to be done. I discovered I would have a hand in helping others go through deliverance and using the apostolic, prophetic, and evangelistic anointing on my life to serve my fellow brothers and sisters in Christ. When Angela Ivory Ministries – AIM was birthed by God to reach lost souls for Christ, but also an extraordinarily strong need for me to help equip the saints. He has appointed some with grace to be Apostles, Prophets, Evangelists, Pastors, or Teachers.

Their calling is to nurture and prepare all the Holy believers to do their own work of ministry so they can enlarge and build the Kingdom of God. I have been knowing and I understand "... *The Spirit of the Lord is upon me, and he has anointed me to be hope for the poor, healing for the brokenhearted, and new eyes for the blind, and to preach to prisoners, 'You are set free!' I have come to share the message of Jubilee, or the time of God's great acceptance has begun (Luke 4:18-19* ***TPT****).*"

"[11] And he has appointed some *with grace* to be apostles, and some *with grace* to

be prophets, and some *with grace* to be
evangelists, and some *with grace* to be
pastors, and some *with grace* to be teachers.
12 And their calling is to nurture and prepare
all the holy believers to do their own works
of ministry, and as they do this they will
enlarge and build up the body of Christ. 13
These grace ministries will function until we
all reach oneness into the faith, until we all
experience the fullness of what it means to
know the Son of God, and finally we
become one into a perfect man with the full
dimensions of spiritual maturity and fully
developed into the abundance of Christ. 14

And then our immaturity will end! And we
will not be easily shaken by trouble, nor led
astray by novel teachings or by the false
doctrines of deceivers who teach clever lies.
15 But instead we will remain strong and
always sincere in our love as we express the
truth. *All our direction and ministries will
flow* from Christ and lead us deeper into
him, the anointed Head of his body, the
church. 16 For his "body" *has been formed in
his image* and is closely joined together and
constantly connected as one. And every
member *has been given divine gifts* to
contribute to the growth of all; and as *these*

gifts work effectively throughout the whole body, we are built up and made perfect in love (Eph. 4:11 – 16 ***TPT***)."

Chapter Seven

Enough is enough.

Throughout this book, I have shared experiences on my journey of knowing that God has called me to be a part of the end time leader. As you can see or have read, I have had much opposition. It's simply because at my birth, I was assigned by God and given assignments just as you have. While my assignments maybe different than yours, the enemy knew that as well and he has tried everything possible to delay me. But the Lord

"[1]O LORD, I have so many enemies; so many are against me. [3]But you, O LORD, are a shield around me; you are my glory, the one

who holds my head high. [4] I cried out to the LORD, and he answered me from his holy mountain. Interlude [5] I lay down and slept, yet I woke up in safety, for the LORD was watching over me. [6] I am not afraid of ten thousand enemies who surround me on every side. [7] Arise, O LORD! Rescue me, my God! Slap all my enemies in the face! Shatter the teeth of the wicked! [8] Victory comes from you, O LORD. May you bless your people. Interlude (Psalms 3:1, 3 – 8 ***NLT****).”*

I had to constantly keep myself, family and those close to me covered in prayer due to having witch coven meeting up to discuss my downfall. I most certainly do not look like what I have been through. I give God all the honor and praise for that. The enemy has gone so far as to use my husband so that we would not move in unity. The power of agreement is powerful, especially with a husband and a wife. He used a sister in Christ; a powerful woman of God that I love and respected (THE SPIRIT OF SABATOGE WAS OPERATING). I mentioned in a previous chapter that I had many sent by God to walk with me on this journey, however, somehow the enemy would use situations in their life to distract them. They found themselves with their own battles to fight, so they had to war for themselves. Lastly, my family ... My mother never did anything purposely to delay me, but life situations, circumstances, and decisions that were made placed her in certain predicaments. If the love for my mother could get me unfocused, or distracted about certain decisions that were made, it would bring more delays. My mother was a born-again believer, she shared Christ everywhere she went. She loved people and she had an evangelistic anointing. She introduced me to Christ and set a very strong foundation of making sure that I put my trust in the Lord. Her desire was for all of her children to have a personal relationship with the Lord; and we all do.

When I began writing this book, she was still living. As of October 2023, she transitioned to Glory. I have shared with some that the Lord prepared me a very long time ago for whenever my mom would transition. He let me know that I would have great peace. The knowledge of me having this peace happened long ago. I thought she would have transitioned way before 2023. He prepared me before He allowed her to experience and me to witness what the last ten years of her would be like. Up until the day she passed away, my mother was blessed and favored by the Lord. She gave Him all glory, honor, and praise. Although she went through a lot of trials in her life; as we all do, He kept her in peace.

Let me explain, so that you will have a better understanding of what happened, and why it's so important that we receive deliverance. God is no respect of persons. There are spiritual laws that we must abide by. We must stand on the precepts of God and not compromise for anything or anyone ...

Ten years ago; in 2013 my father passed away; as I shared in the first chapter. I thank God my husband, our two children, and myself were able to visit him. This was the first time and only time I shared with my dad that Mark needed another kidney. I also mentioned this earlier in the first chapter that my father believed that once a person needed a kidney, they would go on dialysis, and the wait time for some would be so long that they may not survive. Mark never went on dialysis because my husband received a kidney three months after my father passed away, and he's still alive with the perfect match he received. While my father was alive, him and my mother lived in my childhood home even though they were separated. When he passed away, he left my mother living in the residence they purchased back in the 70's. Another family member and their family found themselves in a situation, and they moved back to Louisiana, and moved in with my mother. At first, I thought it was a good idea because she would not be there alone, until after some time, it was revealed to me that if my father would still be alive that this family would not have been allowed to move back into the residence. God has a way of putting people in place to protect you.

KEY – Remember women are covered by God at least three ways if they are married.

Some mothers when dealing with their children sometimes make choices and decisions to help them when they need deliverance. The choices mothers make and the things parent sacrifice for those that are in need of deliverance can sometimes get us in trouble because we are not consulting God first. Many think just because they are family that you are supposed to help no matter what they are going through; I beg to tell you differently. I'm not sure of the conversation that was had, however the first question my mom should have asked God is, "Lord, do You want me step in to help them?" There is nothing wrong with temporary help, however, there comes a time when you need to draw a line. A time limit should have been set; she needed to set boundaries because people will take advantage of you and take your kindness for weakness. At the time of this occurrence, I would have said that she was a very strong woman in the Lord. However, those who are strong in the Lord can be overtaken by other strongholds (spirits) when we open doors that we were not meant to open. At that point, the enemy has legal right to cause havoc in your life. After I noticed what was going on, my mom came to visit for a few weeks. She returned home and we made plans for her to visit again, however, the day before she caught the bus, she passed out. Her health had begun to decline, and she was not the strong woman that she used to be.

Once she was released out of the hospital, we had her to come and visit with us. She lived with us for about a year. During that time, we knew that the house she lived in needed to be vacated and repaired. Two of my brothers and I were trying to help renovate her home, but everything we tried never seemed to work out. At that time a few of our family members left and were able to find their own place however, we still had one brother still living in the house. We tried everything we could to put a plan in place to take care of our mother, but she always seemed to be drawn back. The Holy Spirit told me to release her. I took her back home, and my oldest brother and his wife had mom live with them for a few months.

Eventually, they had to release her and take her back to her home.

Some months later, I went to visit

home to attend a women's conference in August '21 and I stopped in unexpectedly to visit my mom. I had to really step back, pray, and fight this battle in the Spirit. After speaking and asking this family member to seek God as to where they need to be or where they need to move, they refused. It broke my heart to leave my mom in that condition as her health was declining more and more. A mother's love is something ... We watched our mother protect her child even while living in chaos.

KEY – Never let the love of a person, child, mother, father, sister, husband, or wife get in the way of your discernment to follow Christ. To follow Christ, it may require you to let them go; after all, they belong to Him.

It was not even two weeks that passed, it was few days before August 29, 2021, my mother and the other family member had to move out of the home because of hurricane Ida. This happened two years before my mother passed. As I looked back on this, I also saw the hand of the enemy, however the spirit of delay and stagnation was on her life as well. I found out she did not finish pursuing Biblical studies with the church she was connected to. This was another distraction for the enemy to try to delay me, instead, it catapulted me to be the woman of God I am. I had to stay in prayer about this situation, but I could not allow even the situation about my mother to change my course; it actually pushed me. I had to remain focused and recognize the strategy of the enemy ... Just as I recognized different spirits within others, I could also see them within my family. This one hit very close to home y'all, because it is family we're talking about, and my mother was entangled in this mess! The spirit of offense was working overtime.

We were at the end of the year, headed into a year of RELEASE and the enemy was trying to trip me up with offense. You know he is the accuser of the brethren; at any time, he can bring charges to the Father about you. If you open a door to sin (if you miss the mark) you have just given him legal right.

KEY – It was released by another servant of God, and I believe this is the year of release. I am believing God will release so much in 2024 ... A Release of Finances; A Release of from debt; A Release of healing; A Release of revival; A Release of His Anointing; A Release of Greater Glory; A Release of Impartation; A Release of deliverance; and much more.

I had to snap out of it and ask the Lord to forgive me for almost falling into his trap. The Holy Spirit reminded me of the scripture that says, *"[10] When you forgive this man, I forgive him, too. And when I forgive whatever needs to be forgiven, I do so with Christ's authority for your benefit, [11] so that Satan will not outsmart us. For we are familiar with his evil schemes (2 Corinthians 2:10-11* ***NLT).****"*

"[165] There is such a great peace and well-being that comes to the lovers of your Word,

and they will never be offended (Psalms 119:165 ***TPT****).”*

KEY – NO ONE is beyond falling for Satan's traps, whether you have a title or not. Repent quickly and don’t fall for the same trap. You have got to strive to do better. It reminds me of Jesus and the journey He was on. If the enemy knew that killing Him or trying to kill Him, would lead Him to be the ultimate sacrifice, he would have just left Him alone. It is okay, go ahead and Laugh out loud! If the enemy only knew that if I had to endure this type of pain, trial, and pass the test, he would have left me alone!

Several things happened to my mom after my father passed away. In the earlier chapters I talked about women being covered three ways, especially if we are married ... First by God; secondly by your husband; and lastly by a spiritual covering. If the latter of the two are not in position, you are still covered by God. Our mother was diagnosed with dementia (dementia is the loss of memory and judgement). Even after several times of her being cared for by others in their homes, she was drawn back to her house. The reason why is because the stronghold (spirit) wanted her to renew the covenant and stay. However, this time, she was placed in a nursing home a year after leaving Louisiana after the storm because she developed an ulcer; and while she was in the nursing home, she developed gangrene. I must admit that if this would have happened to my mom several years ago, I would have made the foolish mistake of taking her back in to live with us. Because of my growth and trust in God, I knew it was better to follow His plan. I had to trust God and believe He would still take care of her. He told me and my brother, "Release her and take her back home because she is My daughter." Yes, she was our mother, but these are the types of things I'm speaking of when I say you have to ask God to direct you and lead.

KEY – Sometimes you will not understand. Sometimes others will not understand. Sometimes you will look like a fool. It is always better to obey the Lord's instructions despite what anyone else may think.

I was just beginning to get the point in my life where God was breaking off the enemy's grip that had been trying to keep holding me and my family up in several areas of our lives. I was at the point in my spiritual life where I recognized it and would not allow anything, or any circumstance to stand in my way. The enemy is very cunning and if he cannot get you in one area, he will try to reach you by any means necessary. He does not fight fair ... So, instead of being pulled away from what God was already leading me to do in my own personal life, the plan and strategy was to trust and believe Him that everything even with my family would work out for the good. One of the scriptures my mom gave me when I left home at the age of nineteen was, *"5 Trust in the LORD with all thine heart; and lean not unto thine own understanding. 6 In all thy ways acknowledge him, and he shall direct thy paths (Proverbs 3:5-6* ***KJV)****."* I never forgot that scripture because it was vitally important for me trust in the Lord no matter how it felt or what it looked like. And this I know: "[25]*One day when large groups of people were walking along with him, Jesus turned and told them,* [26]*"Anyone who comes to me but refuses to let go of father, mother, spouse, children, brothers, sisters—yes, even one's own self! —can't be my disciple.* [27]*Anyone who won't shoulder his own cross and follow behind me can't be my disciple Luke 14:25-27* ***MSG)****."*

KEY– We must realize and get to a point to know that the good, the bad, and those things that seem ugly, are being used to work for our good even when it does not seem like it or make sense. Even if I would have known my mother would be going on to Glory in October, I still would not have done anything differently. I did what the Lord instructed me for me to do for while she was alive. For some this may be difficult to understand, but the Word says, *"29 And everyone who has given up houses or brothers or sisters or father or mother or children or property, for my sake, will receive a hundred times as much in return and will inherit eternal life "Matthew 19:29* ***NLT)."*** While on this journey, I learned to set my face like flint.

Now let me get to the part when "enough was enough" which was when I started to learn more about biblical and generational curses. I know you guys are probably saying in earlier chapters this girl has bounced from one church to another; but all my moves were orchestrated by the Lord. I went in places I needed to go in order to learn what I needed to learn.

Because of the original sin in the garden, unfortunately we have inherited some biblical curses we are not aware of, and generational issues in our bloodline. The only way these curses will stop operating in our lives is if someone in the bloodline breaks them. You can be the curse breaker in your bloodline. A spiritual repairer of the breach is one that restores correctly; however, you must begin with yourself.

KEY - *"Some of you will rebuild the deserted ruins of your cities. Then you will be known as a rebuilder of walls and a restorer of homes (Isaiah 58:12* ***NLT****)."*

DOUBLE KEY – THE BREAKER'S ANOINTING

"And it shall come to pass in that day, that his burden shall be taken away from off thy shoulder, and his yoke from off thy neck, and the yoke shall be destroyed because of the anointing (Isaiah 10:27 ***KJV****)."*

Let us get back on track ... In the time frame when my mother was admitted to the nursing home for a ulcer (A decubitus ulcer). I still don't understand how this occurred, because she was up, walking, and moving around. However, there were probably some details that were not shared, and the Lord did not allow me to know. Although I may not have known the complete situation of her living conditions, the Lord opened the door for physical therapy to come in and start taking care of her, which is when the ulcer was discovered.

Even then God was answering my prayers, remember I told you I had to just step back and pray about the situation. My mother was very protective of this family member. She was first sent and admitted into the hospital and released to a skilled nursing facility to complete the healing process of the ulcer. While she was there the wound nursed discovered that she had a black spot on her right great toe; which indicated there was an issue with blood flow. The situation got worse, and started affect other toes. The diagnosis was gangrene. In the process, it brought my mother back to the memory of my Great Aunt Lillian. She was diagnosed with a rare disease that caused her to have her fingers and I believe her toes amputated.

My mother then, tried to use her cell phone to call back home (504) in Louisiana. Instead, she kept calling me because I was #5 in her phone on speed dial. She said, "I'm trying to make a long-distance call to someone back at home." She said, "I was not trying to reach you Angela." I was like, "Well mom, you're in Texas and no one is at your residence, so who are you trying call?" The Holy Ghost revealed to me that she was trying to call her Aunt Lillian. At first, I will tell you the fighter in me began to pray. I was thinking that she was seeing familiar spirits, but I realized that she had not been speaking to her, but she was trying to physically talk to her.

Shortly after she had the procedure on her leg to open up the blood vessels, the doctor of course was talking about amputation. The only thing I could think of is that she was trying to reach her Aunt Lillian because she remembered that her aunt's fingers and toes were missing. It was just her short-term memory that had been affected by this spirit of dementia. Our mother did not have issues with her long-term memory, so I assumed that was why she was trying to reach her aunt. I began to have a conversation with my oldest brother Herman about mom trying to reach her aunt. He reminded me why Aunt Lillian's fingers and toes were missing – she had leprosy. Yes. You read it correctly ... leprosy. The government was using her as an experiment to figure out how she was still living with leprosy. I began to ask questions ... The first question I asked was, "Why did Aunt Lillian have leprosy? I went back to the generational thing. Some things happened our lives because of what happened in our bloodline, and it can affect our lives.

I did some research, and there were several people in the Bible who had leprosy, but the one person, Miriam (Moses and Aaron's older sister) stood out to me. Case and point; Miriam came up against Moses. I did not know how God was going to do it, but I was believing God to heal my mother. As I read the scripture, it gave me more strategy on how pray for my mother. Not only was I praying for my mother, my church family that I am connected to was also praying and believing for her healing. I shared with them that she had an issue with gangrene on her toes. They had no idea about my aunt or what happened in our family. As you can see, I did not know this information until I dug a little deeper.

Herman reminded me that Aunt Lillian was a praying woman. Although she was a praying woman, there was a reason why she had leprosy. She may not have always been a praying woman and could have been dealing with a generational curse. Aunt Lillian may have been a partaker of this curse because of her ancestors. I spoke earlier about the strongholds that overtook my mother when the family moved into her home over the years. I am sure that a lot of negative things were said about me because I did not respond or react to their needs as they thought I should. I am not sure what my mother may have come in agreement with, but it could have been a very strong possibility that this had occurred. Even still, I had to trust God. The scripture says: *"While they were at Hazeroth, Miriam and Aaron criticized Moses because he had married a Cushite woman. [2] They said, "Has the LORD spoken only through Moses?*

Hasn't he spoken through us, too?" But the
LORD heard them. [3] *(Now Moses was very*
humble—more humble than any other
person on earth.) [4] *So immediately the LORD*
called to Moses, Aaron, and Miriam and
said, "Go out to the Tabernacle,[a] *all three*
of you!" So the three of them went to the
Tabernacle. [5] *Then the LORD descended in*
the pillar of cloud and stood at the entrance
of the Tabernacle.[b] *"Aaron and Miriam!"*
he called, and they stepped forward. [6] *And*
the LORD said to them, "Now listen to what I
say: "If there were prophets among you, I,
the LORD, would reveal myself in visions.

*I would speak to them in dreams. [7] But not
with my servant Moses. Of all my house, he
is the one I trust. [8] I speak to him face to
face, clearly, and not in riddles! He sees the
LORD as he is. So why were you not afraid to
criticize my servant Moses?" [9] The LORD
was very angry with them, and he departed.
[10] As the cloud moved from above the
Tabernacle, there stood Miriam, her skin as
white as snow from leprosy.[c] When Aaron
saw what had happened to her, [11] he cried
out to Moses, "Oh, my master! Please don't
punish us for this sin we have so foolishly
committed. [12] Don't let her be like a stillborn*

baby, already decayed at birth.” [13] *So Moses cried out to the LORD, “O God, I beg you, please heal her!”* [14] *But the LORD said to Moses, “If her father had done nothing more than spit in her face, wouldn’t she be defiled for seven days? So keep her outside the camp for seven days, and after that she may be accepted back.”* [15] *So Miriam was kept outside the camp for seven days, and the people waited until she was brought back before they traveled again (Numbers 12:1-15* ***NLT****).”*

You are probably saying that people hardly contract leprosy in this age and time, however, it is curable in the early stages to avoid disability. Even though Aunt Lillian had leprosy, her end result was not death; she lost her fingers and her toes to this disease ... The end result for our mom would have been amputation, BUT NOT ON MY WATCH!! I was in total agreement with my mother NOT to have her leg amputated. As I was currently writing June 9th, 2023; I was five days in for praying "Lord heal my mother" and I was two days away from the actual physical manifestation. IN JESUS NAME. WHEWWWW!! I know this seems like a lot, but God made this so very clear to me after my mother passed October 2023. After praying that prayer, and using the example of what God told Moses, my mother was healed. Her gangrene cleared up, but not completely, but it was healing. She had a second surgery to open up her blood vessels once she returned to Louisiana in September of 2023; there was NO need for amputation.

We had been working on ways to get help to renovate our mother's home so that she would have a place to move back to. We received some assistance for this project, but we never received enough money to complete the renovation.

The time came for her to leave the nursing home in Texas. It is so amazing the way God works. He told me to call my brother Larry that lives in Louisiana and share with him what He told me. "It was time to get mom and bring her to Louisiana. She is to stay with him and his family for one month. Then I'm to clear my schedule so Mark and I could get her in October for a month to give you a break." I did not call my brother that night, however, the very next morning the nursing facility called and told me that we needed to prepare to have other living arrangements. She could no longer stay in the facility because she still had Louisiana insurance. We did not want to forfeit her insurance to get Texas insurance and possibly be denied. After I received that phone call, I shared with my brother Larry what God told me.

I just wanted to make sure I was not making any emotional decisions. I wanted to make sure I was hearing from God clearly. I asked my brother to pray about it and let me know.

I believe he called me the next day. We put a plan in action to get our mom out of that facility. My oldest brother Herman was the first leg of the race. He lives in San Antonio. Him and his wife, Norma, picked mom up in Houston. They brought her back to Louisiana to live with my brother Larry his wife until we could get other arrangements made. The second and third leg of the race, my sister-in-law LeDiedra started our mom with a in-home boot camp with weights. They also had home healthcare come out to evaluate her and get the process going to get her back to a normal routine. Thirty days passed by, and Mark and I met my brother halfway in Alabama so we could make the exchange for the fourth leg of the race. She was coming to stay with us for thirty days ... so we thought.

I don't know about you, but if you have had dealings with our Heavenly Father, He does not always tell you everything. Our mother was with us for thirty days, and in the last three weeks of her life, God answered my prayers. When I saw my mother last in Louisiana, I was heartbroken at the condition of her home, and the conditions she was living in. As I said, He answered my prayers. I saw her walk again, and she began to remember some things that were not long-term memory events. We laughed; we went to the Georgia fair; we ate; we sang; we danced, and we prayed at home together. The very first thing God did, He had my spiritual covering pray for our mom and her family the very next day she arrived in Georgia.

Remember I told you women are triple covered. I am thankful for my spiritual covering and that he prayed for my mom two weeks prior to her transitioning. The day she arrived in Georgia, I said, "Mom we have got to get ready for tomorrow, because we will be going to church." That makes me laugh because now I was the one leading her to church for fellowship. She simply said, "Okay church!"

The first Sunday, she could not stand and worship, but the next week, she was able to stand while we did worship. This was one of the things the Lord allowed me to witness before He called her home; the fourth Sunday in October. When I said the Lord answered my prayers, He answered my prayers. He did not allow her to leave this earth in the condition I saw her last in

Louisiana. The Lord also allowed me to see my mother dancing in a field the Friday before she transitioned. It made more sense to me of what I saw after she passed. He was showing me and telling me that she ready to go to her Heavenly home and that I should not stand in her way. She transitioned that Sunday morning in her sleep.

This leads me to most important part of this book ... The children of God need to know that they must always follow the Lord's instructions and never put anyone or anything before Him. Let no one lead or guide your decisions; not mother; not father; not children or friends, because your love for people can make you run the risk of making them an idol. It makes it difficult for you to tell them, NO! It may seem harsh, but it is a life and death situation. Your love for people can dim your discernment. No one is exempt from needing deliverance.

KEY – First we have to admit to spiritual adultery, which is nothing more than being unfaithful to God; loving the things of this world more than the things of God. Through knowledge, the just shall be delivered.

Chapter Eight

Keys to deliverance.

“What is causing the quarrels and
fights among you? Don’t they come from the
evil desires at war within you? 2 *You want*
what you do not have, so you scheme and
kill to get it. You are jealous of what others
have, but you cannot get it, so you fight and
wage war to take it away from them. Yet you
do not have what you want because you do
not ask God for it. 3 *And even when you ask,*
you do not get it because your motives are
all wrong—you want only what will give you
pleasure. 4 *You adulterers! Don’t you realize*
that friendship with the world makes you an
enemy of God? I say it again: If you want to

be a friend of the world, you make yourself
an enemy of God. 5 *Do you think the*
Scriptures have no meaning? They say that
God is passionate that the spirit he has
placed within us should be faithful to him. 6
And he gives grace generously. As the
Scriptures say, "God opposes the proud but
gives grace to the humble." 7 *So humble*
yourselves before God. Resist the devil, and
he will flee from you. 8 *Come close to God,*
and God will come close to you. Wash your
hands, you sinners; purify your hearts, for
your loyalty is divided between God and the
world. 9 *Let there be tears for what you have*

done. Let there be sorrow and deep grief. Let there be sadness instead of laughter, and gloom instead of joy. [10] *Humble yourselves before the Lord, and he will lift you up in honor (James 4:1 – 10* ***NLT****)."*

You must understand there is a spiritual world that is unseen with the natural eye. It is important to stand in prayer and come against the enemy's agenda because along with his cohorts, they are trying to destroy lives. He wants the children of God to remain ignorant to his tactics, schemes, plots, and plans he uses. If we stay prayerful, in the secret place of the

Most High. He will protect and show you things you should pray for or pray against.

It is important we understand the difference between conviction and condemnation. The enemy condemns you of the things you have done in the past and continually brings them before you, until you break the legal rights he has. Even after you break the legal right he has, in his craftiness, he will still try to accuse you, even after repenting and renouncing the sin; falling short of the Glory of God. It is in the "knowing that you are free." Conviction is from the Holy Spirit. He will convict you when you are wrong, but He will not beat you up. He is so full of love, grace, and long suffering. He is also a God of justice, so we all have an end to His grace; a God decision. Thank You Jesus!! He will send warning. We must be open and listen.

A Few Steps to Deliverance.

1. True repentance

You must not only be sorrowful for sin or sinning, but you also want to turn completely away from it; not to go back to it again. *"For all have sinned and come short of the glory of God (Romans 3:23* ***KJV****)."*

You will be tested. You will know you have overcome what once had you bound by passing the test. There are times when I was tested and passed with flying colors. The Holy Spirit would bring it to my attention when I least expect it. I did not get tripped up, which let me know I was FREE of whatever I was tested on.

2. *Confession of sin – Psalms 51*

We must be able to be honest. If we cannot be honest with God, who else can we be honest with? God knows everything; however, we still must confess. It is God alone we have sinned against. If you feel the need to turn to a trusted vessel ...

"*Confess your faults one to another, and pray one for another, that ye may be healed. The effectual fervent prayer of a righteous man availeth much (James 5:16 **KJV**).*"

3. *Honesty*

If you find you need help with your deliverance, being completely honest with the person you are confessing your faults will help. If this vessel has already been tested, you should be comfortable releasing the truth to them. Do not allow the enemy to hide. You do not have to go to someone else to receive deliverance, unless it is something you have been dealing with that will not break. If this is the case, I suggest you go to someone you trust and has the power and authority to get to the root of the matter. All you need to do is repent, renounce, and speak the Word of God over yourself.

4. True Forgiveness

"Forgive those who trespass against us ..." is a part of the model prayer which is a prayer prototype. This is major because if we cannot forgive others, we cannot come before God and ask for forgiveness. We must lay aside every ounce of offense. God knows and sees all, so He will give you justice, but its best to let Him handle it. Nothing goes unnoticed by God. The justice may not happen when you think it should; justice will happen right on time. The unwillingness to forgive will hinder your prayer for deliverance and all of your prayers.

5. Humility/Submission

Pride is a dangerous thing. Be willing to set aside all prideful things in your heart and mind. We must be as submissive as Naaman was in 2 Kings 5. If he had not listened to those around him, he could have missed his deliverance. I used this same word as an example to encourage a sister in Christ before she passed away. I genuinely believe if she would not have been so prideful and listened to the instruction/warning she would still be with us. I am sure there are others just like me who could not put their finger on things; seeing different spirits, and not having an understanding that many needed deliverances. Because of all I was seeing and encountering, I became hungry to learn more and not remain ignorant.

"Lest Satan should get an advantage of us: for we are not ignorant of his devices (2 Corinthians 2:11 ***KJV)****."*

If you seek Him, He will show you great and mysterious things which you still do not know about.

"Call to Me and I will answer you and tell you [and even show you] great and mighty things, [things which have been confined and hidden], which you do not know and

*understand and cannot distinguish (Jeremiah 33: 3 **AMP**).*"

6. *Holiness*

The Word says He is Holy therefore we should want to be holy. There are things you should want to leave behind in your life you cannot be dictated by your flesh, and think you are going to be covered by God. Dying daily to your flesh is necessary. "[13] *Do not offer any part of yourself to sin as an instrument of wickedness, but rather offer yourselves to God as those who have been brought from death to life; and offer every part of yourself to him as an instrument of righteousness.* [14] *For sin shall no longer be your master, because you are not under the law, but under grace (Romans 6:13-14* ***NIV****).*"

Chapter Nine

How to be delivered.

Depending on your family history, there are some curses that have been placed upon us because of our bloodline. We get these curses honestly, if we are not taught better when growing up the enemy has a field day and desires to sift us as wheat. When we are born, his goal is to get us as far away from knowing what our purpose is as possible.

Once we crossed over into this sinful world, we must fight to get back to the conversation God had with each of us before we were formed in our mother's wound. *"I knew you before I formed you in your mother's womb. Before you were born, I set you apart and appointed you as my prophet to the nations (Jeremiah 1:5* ***NLT).****"* Although the Lord is speaking of His prophet Jeremiah, you must know that you too are your own prophet. There are some things we have done to cause a separation in our relationship with God; we cannot blame everything on our ancestors.

I have wonderful news for you ... The Lord loves us and wants to restore His relationship with us when we stray away.

I HAVE A FEW WORDS FOR YOU ...

REPENT – Ask for forgiveness. Ask for forgiveness for those in your family – your ancestors that are no longer here but did not repent and brought those things to the grave that are unresolved. Repentance is not a bad word. We can repent about something every day. The powerful thing about repentance is that it BREAKS the legal right of satan.

RENOUNCE – Simply come out of agreement with; break ties with whatever the sin is.

SPEAK BETTER THINGS – speak the Word of God over your life, family and every situation.

KEY – Please let me explain this to you, expect retaliation/push back from the enemy when you are standing in the gap and praying for other family members, friends; especially if they are family members in the same household. You may not see change in them happening immediately or right away, however it will happen. You must be persistent and this what I meant when I said, "IT IS IN YOUR KNOWING." You have to know because you have prayed, you are praying, and you are praying these prayers in proxy for them that God has heard and will answer, no matter what it looks like, or how much that person is retaliating against you (it is backlash from the enemy's camp)

Just KNOW that God is in control, so release your prayers to Him and have a grateful attitude toward God, because He will NOT fail you. He has NEVER LOST A BATTLE! The Lord has pointed out a few issues His children struggle with. One is idolatry; idols in your life. Anything, any activity, or any person you put before/in front or value the opinions of more than God is an idol. Ask Him to show you what idol (s) you may have. Another issue is having soul ties. Whether it is sexual or in relationships, soul ties are not ordained by God.

KEY – You must be aware of any idols. You must be aware of curses and know that they do exist. Learn about the marine kingdom; marine spirits. You must break all soul ties; put away all idols; and know how to free yourself and from family curses.

Whether it is biblical, generational sin that you or someone in your family has committed and are unaware that it is holding you or family members stagnant. You can be the bloodline breaker. Many will not like this, but any vow or pledge you make to any organization like a fraternity, sorority, or freemasonry is worshipping another deity. The practice of yoga (ALL the poses are moves that are worshipping - giving homage to another god); it is not just exercise. Praying to the universe or a Christian sorority or fraternity are all wrong. The enemy has so many fooled. It is not an acceptable excuse that you are a part of these organizations to do good in your community. You can do good things in your community with your sisters and brothers in Christ. **44** *Now all who believed were together, and had all things in common, 45 and [o] sold their possessions and goods, and divided[p] them among all, as anyone had need Acts 2:43-45* ***NJKV).*** *"*

DOUBLE KEY – I have nothing to lose by saying or writing these things. On this journey, I am ok with walking alone; it is a part of it. If you find yourself getting upset with me because of what you just read about fraternities, sororities, and yoga, you need to check that spirit of pride and insecurity that just manifested. If you must go through everything you went through just to be a part of a brotherhood or sisterhood, even after leaving college, it may have something to do with a void that may have been in your life, or to fit in. You are already a part of a brotherhood and sisterhood if you are in the body of Believers. They should be able cover you in prayer and look out for you if you need anything. I am sharing all these things because I am led by the Holy Ghost to share. The Lord wants you to be free and not be duped by the enemy. Christ paid the full price to set us free from the curse of the law. *"13 Yet, Christ paid the full price to set us free from the curse of the law. He absorbed the curse completely as he became*

a curse in our place. For it is written: 'Everyone who hung upon a tree is Cursed.'
[14]Jesus Christ dissolved the curse from our lives, so that in him all the blessings of Abraham can be poured out upon gentiles.

*And now through faith we receive the promised Holy Spirit who lives in us (Galatians 3:13 – 14 **TPT**).*"

This does not absolve us from understanding you are still under biblical curses, but He has given us power and the authority to cancel or reverse the curses.

BIBLICAL CURSES

Because of the sin in the garden, we inherited curses through our family that goes back to when Eve and Adam. We must break them so that they will stop working in our lives; and teach others as well. Your desire should be to break the cycles so you will not continue to go in circles.

IDOLS

God is a jealous God.

An idol can be a person, or things, or even a promise that God has given you. You can love these things more than your obedience to God. Sometimes the promises God has promised you can become an idol because you are so worried about it coming to pass, that you lose sight of the other things God would have you to focus on; now it has become an idol. "5 *You must not bow down to them or worship them, for I, the LORD your God, am a jealous God who will not tolerate your affection for any other gods. I lay the sins of the parents upon their children; the entire family is affected—even children in the third and fourth generations of those who reject me.* [6] *But I lavish unfailing love for a thousand generations on those who love me and obey my commands (Exodus 20:5 –6* ***NLT****).”*

Ask the Lord to forgive you (and your ancestors, going back 10 generations on both sides of your bloodline) for the sins and iniquities that allowed these curses to come upon you. There may be many of you that prayed prayers; prayed the Word; fasted and prayed, but still continue to go in cycles. You must get to the root of the problem.

“[40] But at last my people will confess their
sins and the sins of their ancestors for
betraying me and being hostile toward me.
[41] When I have turned their hostility back on
them and brought them to the land of their
enemies, then at last their stubborn hearts
will be humbled, and they will pay for their
sins. [42] Then I will remember my covenant
with Jacob and my covenant with Isaac and
my covenant with Abraham, and I will
remember the land. [43] For the land must be
abandoned to enjoy its years of Sabbath rest
as it lies deserted. At last, the people will
pay for their sins, for they have continually

rejected my regulations and despised my decrees. [44] *"But despite all this, I will not utterly reject or despise them while they are in exile in the land of their enemies. I will not cancel my covenant with them by wiping them out, for I am the LORD their God (Leviticus 26:40 – 44* ***NLT****)."*

Chapter Ten

Freedom in Christ.

The key to staying delivered is to maintain a holy life. *Because it is written, Be ye holy; for I am holy (1 Peter 1:16* ***KJV****)."* *AND "*[5]*It is for freedom that Christ has set us free. Stand firm, then, and do not let yourselves be burdened again by a yoke of slavery (Galatians 5:1* ***NIV****)."*

It is so important after you receive deliverance of any issue, it is important to keep your 'house' clean by living a life of holiness. The Holy Spirit can give you the power to live a holy life. He will keep you if you want to be kept.

Many think they lose out by living a holy life. There is peace, joy, freedom, and fun in obeying the Holy Spirit, and living up to the standards of God. You must keep the Blood of Jesus applied to any area you have received deliverance in. *"[43]When an evil spirit leaves a person, it goes into the desert, seeking rest but finding none. [44] Then it says, 'I will return to the person I came from.' So, it returns and finds its former home empty, swept, and in order. [45] Then the spirit finds seven other spirits more evil than itself, and they all enter the person and live there. And so that person is worse off than before. That will be the experience of this evil generation (Matthew 12:43 – 45* ***NLT****)."* Live a holy life with a pure heart. It does not mean that you will never have challenges. If you allow the Holy Spirit to lead, guide, and rule your life whenever something tries to get into your heart that is not like God. Uproot every sickness, disease, sin, and ungodly covenants by the Blood of Jesus. Apply the Word of God to any and every situation you have. The Word is sharper than any two-edged sword.

Chapter Eleven

Praying prayers for other's deliverance.

To pray for someone else's deliverance, you must know how to engage in spiritual warfare. When you are standing in the gap for your family and others, make sure you cover yourself with the Armor of God. "[10] *A final word: Be strong in the Lord and in his mighty power.* [11] *Put on all of God's armor so that you will be able to stand firm against all strategies of the devil.* [12] *For we are not fighting against flesh-and-blood enemies, but against evil rulers and authorities of the unseen world, against mighty powers in this dark world, and against evil spirits in the heavenly places.* [13]

Therefore, put on every piece of God's
armor so you will be able to resist the enemy
in the time of evil. Then after the battle you
will still be standing firm. 14 *Stand your*
ground, putting on the belt of truth and the
body armor of God's righteousness. 15 *For*
shoes, put on the peace that comes from the
Good News so that you will be fully
prepared. 16 *In addition to all of these, hold*
up the shield of faith to stop the fiery arrows
of the devil. 17 *Put on salvation as your*
helmet, and take the sword of the Spirit,
which is the word of God. 18 *Pray in the*
Spirit at all times and on every occasion.

Stay alert and be persistent in your prayers for all believers everywhere (Ephesians 6:10 – 18 ***NLT****).* "

It is important to get delivered BEFORE standing in the gap. It is not wise or effective to try to point out other's sin before dealing with the sin within yourself or your family. The enemy will have a field day with you, so get delivered first. When you stand in the gap and break all curses and covenants, renounce all demonic covenants with your mouth for ALL your family to receive total deliverance. You are standing in the gap so that the accuser of the brethren (satan) will not have anything to accuse you or your family of. When praying for your family make sure you call out your family's last name and maiden names on both sides of the family. If you do not know it, research, or ask other family members. For instance, when I was praying for my mother, I found out what my Great Aunt Lillian's last name was. I made sure I covered all bases.

I did not mention in chapter seven when I was able to visit my mother in the nursing facility in Houston, we prayed together, and I led her through some prayers of repentance. This is a testimony of how standing in the gap for your family can and will be successful.

KEY – Even though you are standing in the gap for your loved ones or friends, if they are open and willing to allow you to lead then through some prayers, certainly do so. If they are not open to it, continue to pray for them privately. They do not have to know what you are praying for, but I encourage you to look for signs of victory. Remember IT IS IN THE KNOWING! You need to know that your prayers are being heard and they are being answered, no matter what it looks like or how it may seem. The enemy always puts up a smoke screen before you. His desire is for you to get frustrated and quit. Do not quit ... keep praying and ... PRAISE HIM IN

ADVANCE – YOU HAVE THE VICTORY!

Chapter Twelve

Prayers.

In the name of the Lord Jesus Christ, I bring judgement from the throne of Jesus Christ against every foul power, witchcraft, and curse in the name of JESUS CHRIST. I take my case to the court of heaven and plead guilty on my behalf; and I plead guilty in my ancestor's behalf. Lord forgive us from all sin known and unknown. Lord reveal to me anything that is hidden (If you know of any sin that you have committed or your ancestors have committed, begin to call those things out. For instance, the spirit of anger, the spirit of murder; the spirit of jealousy, the spirit of pornography, spirit of perversion; the spirit of manipulation (witchcraft); the spirit of lying, the spirit of adultery, the spirit of molestation, and so forth). As I bring this case to the courts of Heaven, because of the Blood of Jesus that was shed, our verdict is no longer, Guilty. I decree the accuser of the brethren cannot drudge up and bring up the past of my ancestors or any sin or iniquity I have committed in Jesus' name, because Lord, You said that we are not guilty, and we are free. I renounce and come out of agreement; break all written agreements, verbal agreements, and agreements made in dreams. Every contract I did not know of, I make them powerless. Every witchcraft prayer prayed over myself, my family, and my ancestors; or any involvement my ancestors may have been involved in, I renounce and fall out of agreement with it/them. Any word curses I have spoken over myself or my family, I curse it at the root; I detach myself and my family from it, and I plead the Blood of Jesus over it. I declare and decree The Lord has wonderful things planned for me, plans to prosper me, not plans to harm me, plans of hope and a future. Plans to be completely healed from any sickness, disease, or infirmity. I come in agreement with the plans to prosper in all areas of my life; spiritually, physically, and mentally. In Jesus name I pray. Amen."

The prayer you just read is easy to pray and it does not mean you will not pray the prayer again, because the Holy Spirit can reveal something else to you later. Say for instance you knew you had a problem with masturbation; telling lies and you ask God to forgive you of those things; you repented for them; and renounce them (which means that you fell out of agreement with those things).

Now, you began to speak the Word of God over your life pertaining to that certain area, and the Lord builds you. You may need deliverance at other times once sin, or sins are revealed to you (it may not happen all at the same time). Now that you have the tools that you need to overcome. I suggest that you find a reputable man or woman of God that deals heavily and have experience in deliverance.

Here is a personal prayer I prayed for myself and my family. I did not write this prayer; I just came in agreement with the prayer ...

October 10, 2023, while praying and fasting, I prayed this prayer ...

"Every loss, delay, or disruption that I have ever suffered or am currently suffering because of the operations of this spirit in my life, is hereby underwritten by the Blood of Jesus, through the completed works of Christ on the cross of Calvary.

I break free from every hinderance; I break my family free of every hinderance; I break the church family I am connected to free from every hinderance; I break my destiny free in the name of Jesus.

I receive strength in Christ to move forward in progress and prosperity. I will not be discouraged; I will not be confounded; I will not be dismayed.

I pray for increased sensitivity to the voice and leading of the Holy Spirit and for clarity to understand His promptings.

I pray for God to overturn the table of the adversary and turn their schemes to defraud, rob, or cheat us out of our rightful reward, to be frustrated and annulled in the name of Jesus."

I call forth and pray for the release of the provisions, resources, helpers that are needed in each month for God's counsel and purpose (for October and every month) by calling forth our season/destiny to be fulfilled in Jesus Mighty name!

I thank God in advance and in faith for answering our prayers, and for the miracles, blessings, breakthroughs, testimonies, and victories that the remaining of 2023 will bring into our life, as the Lord tarries.

KEY – Sometimes you may have to just take authority and cast out devils, not necessarily pray. Here is an example ... "I bind and cast out all spirits of fear, anxiety; panic attacks, hypertension, worry, and doubt from you and your family. I plead the Blood of Jesus against all of these from the root which they came in. I close those doors NOW, and seal them with the Blood of Jesus, and send them to Jesus for judgement and forbid them to come back upon you or your family in any, way, shape; or touch anyone else on the way! I loose upon us all Your perfect love for it is perfect love that casts our all fear. In the name of the Lord Jesus Christ, I now bring the fullness of His the cross, His blood, His sacrifice, His resurrection, His life and His empty tomb; His authority, His rule, and His dominion. I bring judgement from the throne of Jesus Christ against every foul power; witchcraft, black art, and curse in the name of Jesus Christ."

The Conclusion

When the Lord made you, He made you with a purpose. He made you a warrior with assignments. God formed you in your mother's womb; and He had a conversation with you. Now that you have read this book, my prayer is that you were remined of this one thing, *"Being confident of this very thing, that he which hath begun a good work in you will perform it until the day of Jesus Christ: (Philippians 1:6* ***KJV****)."* Your purpose may have been delayed, but ***NOT*** denied, ***NOR*** derailed! "And as Jesus told Simon the enemy has asked to sift you as wheat, but I have prayed for you, Simon that your faith does not fail. And when you have turned back, strengthen your brothers." I pray you have been strengthened by the KEYS OF VICTORY. Now, put them to use.

ABOUT THE AUTHOR

ANGELA IVORY
of

Angela Ivory Ministries is a native of Louisiana. She is the daughter of the late Ernest L. Baldwin and Albertine Baldwin. She is the youngest of four children; and the only girl.

She is the wife of Mark Ivory, and mother of two sons; Marques and Marcus.

Angela Ivory is first a daughter and servant of the Most High God. Although the ministry bears her name, she fully understands that Jesus is her source. She accepted her call from God to minster the Gospel in 2013. Her purpose is to target the lost and win souls for Jesus Christ, as well as encourages Believers to be sold out for Christ; and help aid with their healing and deliverance. She is under the leadership of Pastor Melvin Womack and Pastor Julia Womack of End-Time Harvest Christian Center.

Angela has been called to the marketplace in several of the "Seven Mountains of Influence." They are; The mountain of Arts and Entertainment, as an author and media personality; and the mountain of Business; as a chef and entrepreneur.

Angela has been given an assignment by God to host her own TV Show entitled “Destiny Helpers” where she spotlights other destiny helpers that are helping others reach their destiny in their community and beyond. She accepts sponsorships to fund the assignment.

CONTACT INFORMATION

TEXT or CALL – 478 324 3568

To Schedule Engagements

EMAIL:

Angelaivoryministries@yahoo.com

www.ingramcontent.com/pod-product-compliance
Lightning Source LLC
LaVergne TN
LVHW020713110826
845149LV00012B/2247

* 9 7 9 8 9 9 0 8 3 3 7 0 8 *